A GUIDED WORKBOOK

The Compass Within

Stop Playing With Your Potential

Define Your Values & Live Life on Your Terms

Cover Art: Shak
Printed in the United States of America
First Printing: 2025
ISBN Print: 979-8-9987174-0-6

This book is for the ones who've been living by everyone else's rules and finally decided enough is enough.

The ones who've been making decisions about who to love, where to work, how to act... based on values that were never really theirs to begin with.

The ones who feel the pull, knowing that something is off, that life should feel more aligned, more intentional, more YOU.

You've always had a compass inside you.
It's time to learn how to use it.

Getting Started

Define It.

Own It.

Live It.

Before You Begin: Start With Honesty

Years ago, there was a time when people would write their thoughts in diaries. Today, a lot of people are scared to write down their real thoughts. There's this **fear** that if someone ever found those pages, they'd be judged... exposed... maybe even embarrassed. Some of us don't even want to sit still in our own thoughts, let alone say them out loud to a friend, a partner, or a therapist. So they keep their thoughts to themselves.

What most people don't realize is that the fear isn't always about being judged by others, it's about finally having to face ourselves. There's an internal tug of war between who we've been told to be and who we actually are? That's where most of us get stuck! Too afraid to process our feelings, admit to ourselves or to others what we want, let alone go after it.

Then, there's a whole other group: the ones moving through life on autopilot. They're doing what's expected, going to work / school, getting married/ selecting partners, raising kids, checking off boxes, but deep down, they feel empty, unfulfilled or disconnected. Maybe it looks like staying in a job (or relationship) they've outgrown because it's "safe" or "familiar". Or saying yes to things that don't feel good just to avoid rocking the boat. Or waking up one day wondering, "How did I even get here?" That sense of uncertainty you feel, well that's living in survival mode & **surviving isn't the same as living.**

So, if you're holding this guide in your hands it means you already feel like there's more for you. More clarity needed. More purpose. More YOU in your life.

This is **your invitation to go deeper. To get honest about what moves you, identify what matters most, and what's truly non-negotiable in the life you're building.**

A lot of the choices you make, who you date, where you work, where you live, how you show up in relationships are rooted in your **values** (even if you don't realize it). Here's the problem, some of those values weren't even yours to begin with. They were handed to you, by family, by culture, by society and because you never stopped to question them, you've been living by rules that don't fit who you really are.
That stops today.

This guide is here to help you:
- **Uncover the values that actually belong to YOU, not the ones you inherited.**
- **Create boundaries that protect those values.**
- **Recognize the difference between alignment (feeling good, grounded, at peace) and misalignment (that gut feeling that something's off).**

Because when your values are clear, so are your decisions. And when your life aligns with what truly matters to you, everything flows better.

When it doesn't? That's when you feel off-balance, drained, or resentful. So as you move forward with these exercises, don't hold back. **The magic happens when you're honest with yourself.** That's how you stop living for everyone else and finally start living for YOU.

Shak

About The Author

I've accomplished some things before turning 50. I climbed the corporate ladder, spent over 20 years in Talent Acquisition and HR, and helped thousands of people, grow personally, build successful businesses, land jobs and level up their careers. I've been happily married for over 30 years, have a beautiful family, bought my first home before 30, and became a successful real estate investor.

But **none of this happened by chance,** I saw the vision first. I believed in that vision. And more importantly, I believed in **my ability to make it happen. I wasn't gifted anything.** I had to work for ALL of it! None of this happened overnight and it all started with my mindset, how I chose to view the world, my current environment and what I wanted for my life.

I've always been **goal-oriented**, and let me be clear, **I wasn't born into privilege,** *far from it*, that's another book for another time. What I did have was a **strong belief that life had more to offer me,** and I was willing to get over my fear and **put in the work** to get what I wanted.

Was it always easy? **HELL no.**

About The Author

Were there challenges? **Absolutely!**

I had to figure out how to move in spaces that weren't built for me, and still make it work. I had to learn to silence the voice in my head that said I didn't belong in these spaces or couldn't do these things and show up anyway.

Did it feel daunting at times? Yes. But impossible? Never.

I believe people can achieve anything, but first, they have to decide how bad they want it and be willing to do what it takes to get it.

I want you to know that I have lived, breathed, and followed every word in these pages. This process isn't just theory, it's been tested, refined, and proven. I know it works because I've used it again and again. It works IF you put in the work!

Understanding How Values Work

Living for validation

keeps you lost.

Living in alignment

keeps you grounded.

Values: Your Inner Compass

What do you **believe in?**

What do you **stand for?**

What **truly matters** to you?

Your **values** are your **internal compass,** they guide your decisions, shape your beliefs, and ultimately influence the goals you set for yourself. When you move in alignment with your values, life just **feels right.** You're fulfilled, you're clear, and you're walking in your purpose.

But when things in your life **don't** match up with your values? That's when frustration creeps in. You feel **stuck, uneasy, or even lost**, like something is off, and you can't put your finger on it.

Let Me give you an example:

One of my core values is **Community & Impact**. I genuinely **care about helping others grow**. I love to see people **win**, and whenever possible, I've always been the one offering guidance, resources, and tools to help them do just that.

That's why creating this book wasn't just a random idea, it's a **direct reflection of my values.** I wanted to take what I've always done on a personal / professional level and scale it so I can **help even more people step into their power.**

Values: Your Inner Compass

On the other hand, I've held jobs that weren't necessarily aligned with my values.

Sure, the job provided income I needed but I always felt like I was meant to do so much more... That feeling? That was my values talking. I just hadn't learned to listen yet.

So I either ended up staying in jobs longer than I needed (because I was playing it safe) or leaving in a constant pursuit of change but not knowing what I really needed to change.

See how knowing your values connects to the choices you make?

Understanding this is so important. **When you understand your values, decision making becomes easier.** You start moving with clarity, making choices that align with the life you actually **want** to build.

And here's something else, your values might shift as you grow. What mattered to you ten years ago might not hold the same weight today, and that's okay. Self-awareness is key, and checking in with your values is a **lifelong exercise. Let's Get To Work!**

ALIGNED	MISALIGNED
Decisions Feel Clear: You know what to say yes & no to	Everything feels heavy: Even small choices are exhausting
Energy feels full: You're less drained!	Resentment creeps in: You say yes to things and feel worse for it
Relationships feel right: You attract people that get you	Something feels off: You can't name it, BUT you feel it
Purpose feels present: Work and Life feel connected	You're on Autopilot: cruising through life, checking boxes, but not living

On the next few pages, I want you to **reflect and write down what truly matters to you.** If you're unsure where to start, use these prompts to help uncover your values. Take your time with this. Don't rush it.

Prompts to Help You Identify Your Core Values

1. What qualities do I admire in others? (People often don't realize what they value until they see it in someone else.)
2. What makes me feel the most fulfilled and at peace?
3. What am I most passionate about?
4. When have I felt the most proud of myself? What was I doing?
5. What things instantly make me feel uncomfortable, frustrated, or out of alignment? (Discomfort is a clue that something's off. Helps define not just what you stand for, but what you won't tolerate. Things you don't tolerate won't align with your values)
6. If I had to build a life from scratch with no outside opinions, what would be non-negotiable for me? (This helps you think about what you truly want, not what others tell you to want. It's like hitting reset and asking, 'What actually matters to me, even if no one else agrees?')
7. If I could only be remembered for one thing, what would I want it to be?
8. When have I felt like I was betraying myself and what was I compromising?

Defining YOUR
Core Values

Own It

Align It

Live It

Values Exercise

If you're reading these prompts and still feel unsure about how to answer them, don't worry, I got you.

Breaking It Down: How to Think Through These Prompts

I want you to take your time with these questions. **Dig deep.** Don't just think about what sounds good, think about what **feels real** to you. To help guide you, I'm sharing <u>my personal answers</u> (as an example) so you can see exactly how to work through them. Be descriptive - no one-word answers.

Use the lines provided after each prompt to write as much as you need, there are no wrong answers here.

1. What qualities do I admire in others?

(Hint: The things you admire in other people are often a reflection of what you deeply value.)

Example (Me): I admire people who are **authentic, bold, and don't play small (they take risk)**. I love being around people who **speak their truth, go after what they want, and uplift others in the process**. This tells me that I value **authenticity, confidence, and community**.

☑ **Now, think about the people you admire most. These could be people in your life or people you've observed. What is it about them that speaks to you?**

2. What makes me feel the most fulfilled and at peace?
(Hint: Think about the moments in life when you feel truly happy, grounded, and aligned.)

Example (Me): I feel the most fulfilled when I'm **helping people grow**, whether it's through coaching, mentoring, or simply being a resource. I also feel at peace when I have **freedom...freedom of my time to do the things I really want to do. I feel at peace when I have financial freedom, where money isn't a source of stress. I don't have to worry about bills, they are on autopay! I'm at peace when I have the creative freedom to build my life on my terms**.

☑ Now, think about a moment when you felt completely at peace. What were you doing? Who were you with?

3. What am I most passionate about?

(Hint: Passion fuels purpose. Your biggest passions are usually tied to your values.)

Example (Me): I'm passionate about **growth, mine and others**. Whether it's in business, relationships, or mindset, I love **seeing people win and step into their power, especially the ones who were doubted or even doubted themselves, yet were able to overcome their circumstances**. That's why I created this book, because I believe in **giving people tools that help them to move forward**.

☑ Now, what's something you could talk about for hours and never get tired of? What excites you?

4. When have I felt the most proud of myself? What was I doing?

(*Hint: The moments that make you proud show you what's most important to you.*)

Example (Me): I felt the most proud when I **took control of my career and stepped into entrepreneurship**. It was scary, because it required me to bet on me. But it was time. I was working in jobs that weren't aligned with what mattered to me. I realized that I didn't have to stay in spaces that didn't serve me. I could **create my own path**. That moment confirmed that **independence, freedom, and self-reliance** are major values for me.

☑ **Now, think of a time when you accomplished something and felt proud. Why did you feel proud?**

5. What things instantly make me feel uncomfortable, frustrated, or out of alignment?
(Hint: The things that trigger you usually go against your values. Think outside of yourself here — the environments you've been in, the people you've been around, the situations that made you want to walk out of a room or distance yourself from certain people. Your triggers are clues.)

Example (Me): I get frustrated when I'm in environments where people **aren't being real, when there's dishonesty, or when people make excuses for why they can't go after what they want**. Those environments told me everything I needed to know about what I value: honesty, action, and accountability.

☑ **Now, think of a time when something didn't sit right with you. Describe the situation - what felt off?**

6. If I had to build a life from scratch with no outside opinions, what would be non-negotiable for me?
(*Hint: Forget what society, your family, or your friends think. What are the things YOU refuse to live without?*)
Your non-negotiables might look different depending on where you are in life. That's okay. What matters is that they're yours

Example (Me): My **non-negotiables** are **freedom (time, financial, and creative), authenticity, growth, and deep, meaningful connections**. If a job, relationship, or opportunity forces me to shrink myself or give up my independence, it's a NO.

☑ **Now, if you could design your life exactly how you want it, what would you make sure is included? What would you refuse to tolerate?**

7. If I could only be remembered for one thing, what would I want it to be?
(Hint: Your legacy is a reflection of your values.)

Example (Me): I want to be remembered as someone who **pushed people to be their best, live unapologetically, and go after everything they deserve.** If people say, "She made me believe in myself," then I've done what I came here to do.

☑ **Now, what do you want your impact to be? What do you want people to say about you when you're not in the room?**

8. When have I felt like I was betraying myself and what was I compromising? (Hint: This one is different from prompt 5. This isn't about what other people or environments did to you. This is about the moments YOU made a choice that didn't honor who you are. The times you stayed quiet when you should have spoken. Said yes when everything in you said no. Played small to make someone else comfortable. Regret and discomfort are signals, they show you exactly where you abandoned yourself.)

Example (Me): I betrayed myself when I stayed silent to keep the peace, when I doubted my instincts because someone else questioned me, when I shrunk myself to fit spaces that were never built for me. Those were MY choices. And recognizing that was the first step to making different ones. Compromising my voice, my authenticity, and my freedom was never worth it and I made a decision that it never would happen again.

✅ **Think back to a moment when YOU made a choice that didn't align with who you are. Not what someone did to you — what did you do or not do? What value did you compromise in that moment?**

My Values. My Blueprint.

📌 **My Values Recap (Example)**

After going through these prompts, and sharing my personal answers, here's what I know about myself:

I deeply value **authenticity** and **boldness,** not just in myself, but in the people I surround myself with. I'm inspired & drawn to those who show up real, speak their truth, and refuse to play small. I thrive in spaces where **community, connection**, and **growth** are at the center.

Freedom, in how I spend my time, how I earn, and how I express myself is non-negotiable. I've built my life around it and feel most at peace when I'm in control of my time, energy, and direction.

I care deeply about **helping others grow**, which is why I created this book, & why I continue to share what I've learned. Watching someone step into their power? That lights me up.

When things feel out of alignment, it's usually because I'm in spaces where people are being inauthentic, where accountability is lacking, or where people are making excuses instead of taking action. That's when I know I'm in the wrong room. It's draining.

My Values. My Blueprint.

I want to be remembered as someone who showed others what was possible. Someone who lived unapologetically and empowered others to do the same. Someone who inspired people to stop playing with their potential.

Below you'll see my core values. These are mine. You may start with 3 to 5. That's enough to get started

Authenticity	Impact	Accountability
Freedom	Self-Reliance	Confidence
Growth	Integrity	Connection
		Community

These values shape how I make decisions, how I show up, and what I'm building. They are the compass that keeps me aligned and in motion.

✦ Recap: YOUR Core Values at a Glance

You've done the work, peeled back some layers, and got real with yourself. That took courage. Now it's time to pull it all together.

Here's how to complete your recap:

Go back through every prompt you answered.

As you read through your responses look for the words, feelings, and themes that kept showing up. What mattered most in each answer?

What made you feel something when you wrote it? Those recurring themes are your values trying to identify themselves.

Circle them, underline them, highlight them, whatever works for you.

Then use what you've identified to complete the recap on the next page. Write a summary of your values.

Don't overthink it. You've already done the hard part. This is just about naming what's already there.

My Core Values & Why They Matter:

Why this matters:

Your values aren't just something you identify once and forget. They become the filter you run every major decision through. This way, when decisions feel hard you'll know which value is being tested.

When opportunities pop up you'll know which ones are actually aligned with who you are.

When relationships shift you'll understand why certain people drain you and others energize you.

When you feel conflicted you'll be able to name exactly which value is being challenged and that clarity changes everything.

These values are your compass. Come back to them whenever you need to reset, refocus, or realign.

HOW VALUES SHAPE EVERYTHING

YOUR CORE VALUES

DECISIONS
WHAT YOU SAY YES & NO TO

BOUNDARIES
WHAT YOU PROTECT & GUARD

RELATIONSHIPS
WHO YOU ALLOW CLOSE TO YOU

CAREER PATH
WORK THAT DRAINS VS. WORK THAT FUELS

DAILY HABITS
HOW YOU SPEND YOUR TIME & ENERGY

YOUR OVERALL FULFILLMENT

The Alignment Audit: Where Are You Now?

You've done the deep work. You know your values. Now comes the most important question: is the life you're currently living actually reflecting them?

This is where most people stop. They do the work, feel good about what they discovered, and then go right back to living the same way. Don't be that person.

This exercise is simple but it requires you to be honest. No one is grading you. No one is watching. This is between you and you.

Here's how to complete it:

Look at each of the five life areas listed on the next few pages. For each one, think about where you are right now — not where you want to be, not where you used to be. Right now.

Then ask yourself one question: does this area of my life reflect the values I just identified?

If yes — check Aligned. If it needs work — check Needs Work.

Then use the notes section to write down the first honest thought that comes to mind. Don't overthink it. Don't edit yourself. Just write what's real.

There are no wrong answers here.

An honest "needs work" is worth more than a comfortable lie.

The whole point of knowing your values is knowing where to direct your energy and this audit shows you exactly where that is.

Now go deeper on what needs work:
For each area you marked "Needs Work" complete the following.

Be specific — vague answers produce vague results.

The area that needs work:

What specifically feels out of alignment with my values:

The honest reason I haven't addressed it yet:

One small but real step I can take this week:

Alignment Audit

Hold your values up against your real life and see where they actually match

Life Area	Aligned	Needs Work	What's the first honest thing that comes to mind?
Career/work			
Relationships			
Finances			
Personal Growth			
Daily Habits / Lifestyle			

If you found yourself checking 'Needs Work' more than 'Aligned' that's okay.

That's actually the point. You can't build a values-aligned life without first seeing clearly where the gaps are.

What you just did takes more courage than most people ever find. Now you know exactly where to focus.

For each area you marked "Needs Work" use the prompts below to go deeper. Remember, vague answers produce vague results. No one is reading this but you, so be honest with yourself. That honesty is where the real work begins.

The area that needs work:

What specifically feels out of alignment with my values:

The honest reason I haven't addressed it yet:

One small but real step I can take this week:

For each area you marked "Needs Work" use the prompts below to go deeper. Remember, vague answers produce vague results. No one is reading this but you, so be honest with yourself. That honesty is where the real work begins.

The area that needs work:

What specifically feels out of alignment with my values:

The honest reason I haven't addressed it yet:

One small but real step I can take this week:

For each area you marked "Needs Work" use the prompts below to go deeper. Remember, vague answers produce vague results. No one is reading this but you, so be honest with yourself. That honesty is where the real work begins.

The area that needs work:

What specifically feels out of alignment with my values:

The honest reason I haven't addressed it yet:

One small but real step I can take this week:

For each area you marked "Needs Work" use the prompts below to go deeper. Remember, vague answers produce vague results. No one is reading this but you, so be honest with yourself. That honesty is where the real work begins.

The area that needs work:

What specifically feels out of alignment with my values:

The honest reason I haven't addressed it yet:

One small but real step I can take this week:

For each area you marked "Needs Work" use the prompts below to go deeper. Remember, vague answers produce vague results. No one is reading this but you, so be honest with yourself. That honesty is where the real work begins.

The area that needs work:

What specifically feels out of alignment with my values:

The honest reason I haven't addressed it yet:

One small but real step I can take this week:

Personal Reminder
Whenever I feel stuck, overwhelmed, or unsure, I will check back in with these values to make sure the choices I'm making align with who I am and who I'm becoming.

✦ **My Values = My Blueprint.**

Final Thoughts

Your values aren't just words, they shape your decisions, the people you keep around, and the life you build. I hope you took your time with this & was honest with yourself.

Because once you're clear on your values, your goals won't just be dreams anymore. They'll be intentional steps toward the life you're meant to live.

Closing Thoughts & Next Steps

Discover.

Define.

Direct Your

Life.

Looking Back & Moving Forward

People love to talk about what they want, but a lot of times fear keeps them stuck right where they are.

You've already broken that cycle. You didn't just sit with random thoughts floating in your head, you sat down, got real, and did something most people never do. You got clear on what actually matters to you. You identified your values, your non-negotiables, the things that are going to guide every decision you make from this point forward. And most importantly? You moved. You took action.

Pat yourself on the back. You're reinventing yourself. Your values are the one thing that grows with you through every reinvention.

Here's the thing to keep in mind **reinvention isn't optional,** in many ways, it's necessary.

The person you were at 14 years old won't be the same person you are at 20 years old.
- Who you are at 20 isn't meant to carry you at 30.
- Who you are at 30 won't cut it at 40, 50, 60+
- And who you are right now? Is just the foundation for the person you're still becoming.

That's the beauty of knowing your **values,** they grow with you. They evolve, shift, and expand, just like you do. When you're clear on what matters most, you don't cling to the old version of you out of habit. You **release what no longer fits** and make room for what does.

Looking Back & Moving Forward

At some point, you've held onto people, beliefs, and situations that didn't align with who you were becoming, not because they were right for you, but because they were familiar or comfortable.

But now? You know better.

You're done making yourself small to fit spaces that no longer serve you. You're stepping into new opportunities, new choices, and new beginnings, all rooted in values that actually belong to YOU.

You also understand now that life doesn't always play fair, but that's not your measuring stick.

You've been built for this. You've adapted, pushed through, and grown in ways you probably didn't even give yourself credit for.

You've done the inner work. Now the outer work begins. Will every dream come true? Maybe, maybe not.

But you're in the best possible position to chase the ones that actually matter because they're built on YOUR foundation, not someone else's expectations.

Let's Stay Connected:
Share Your Wins & Insights

You know your only real competition is you. So make sure today's version of you is a little wiser, a little stronger, a little clearer than yesterday's. Some days you'll make big moves, other days it's just baby steps, but every step counts.

Most importantly you are **not behind**. You are exactly where you need to be. **Your timeline is yours**. Your values are yours. Your goals, your path, your pace, they all belong to you. And when you stay true to those values, **you'll always be moving in the right direction.**

Time will keep moving with or without you. The only question is: are you moving toward the life YOU deserve?

Now that you know your values, you already have your personal compass. The rest? That's on you. It's up to you, to do something with the knowledge you now have. How far you go is entirely up to you...give yourself permission to soar!

I love to see people win. If this guide has **shifted your mindset, helped you push past your limits, or inspired you to take action, I want to hear about it.**

🔖 **Drop me a message and share your journey!**

📧 Email me at **shakempowers@gmail.com**

Let's celebrate your growth. The compass is yours. Now go use it..